Xtreme Adventure
GHOST HUNTING

BY S.L. HAMILTON

Visit us at
www.abdopublishing.com

Published by ABDO Publishing Company, PO Box 398166, Minneapolis, MN 55439.
Copyright ©2014 by Abdo Consulting Group, Inc. International copyrights reserved in all countries. No part of this book may be reproduced in any form without written permission from the publisher. A&D Xtreme™ is a trademark and logo of ABDO Publishing Company.

Printed in the United States of America, North Mankato, Minnesota.
092013
012014

 PRINTED ON RECYCLED PAPER

Editor: John Hamilton
Graphic Design: Sue Hamilton
Cover Design: Sue Hamilton
Cover Photo: Thinkstock
Interior Photos: Alamy-pgs 10-11; AP-pgs 4-5, 7 (inset) 12-13, 20-23, & 26-27 (bottom); Bourbon Orleans Hotel-pgs 16-17; Corbis-pg 29; Dreamstime-pg 28; iStock-pgs 6-7 & 8-9; Library of Congress-pg 22 (inset); Matt Smith-pgs 18-19; Thinkstock-pgs 1, 2-3, 14-15; 18 (inset), 24-25, 26-27 (top); 30-32; Winchester Mystery House-pgs 10 (inset) & 11 (inset).

ABDO Booklinks
Web sites about Xtreme Adventures are featured on our Book Links pages. These links are routinely monitored and updated to provide the most current information available.
Web site: www.abdopublishing.com

Library of Congress Control Number: 2013946158

Cataloging-in-Publication Data

Hamilton, S.L.
 Ghost hunting / S.L. Hamilton.
   p. cm. -- (Xtreme adventure)
Includes index.
ISBN 978-1-62403-211-0
1. Ghosts--Juvenile literature.   2. Haunted places--Juvenile literature. 3. Parapsychology--Juvenile literature.   I. Title.
133.1--dc23

                              2013946158

CONTENTS

Ghost Hunting 4

Tools & Equipment 6

Dangers 8

Haunted Houses .10

Ghost Hotels 14

Haunted Hospitals 18

Battlegrounds 22

Ships 26

Cemeteries 28

Glossary 30

Index 32

GHOST HUNTING

Some people say there are no such things as ghosts. Others are sure these spirits of the dead are real. They describe ghosts in many different ways. Some ghosts make loud moans and howls, while others are quiet. Some have clear shapes, while others are light wisps of smoke. Some ghosts seem friendly, while others are terrifying.

XTREME FACT– Ghosts are also called spirits, wraiths, specters, apparitions, phantoms, and spooks.

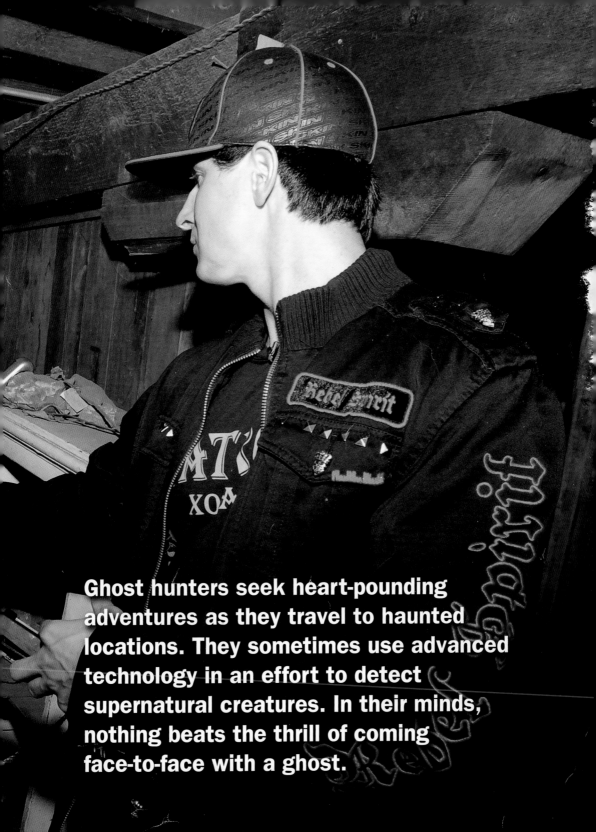

Ghost hunters seek heart-pounding adventures as they travel to haunted locations. They sometimes use advanced technology in an effort to detect supernatural creatures. In their minds, nothing beats the thrill of coming face-to-face with a ghost.

TOOLS & EQUIPMENT

Ghost hunters use temperature-sensing equipment, such as thermal scanners and thermometers to find cold spots. These cool areas could be a ghostly presence. A thermal image shows the shape and size of a cold mass.

Ghost hunters also use motion detectors, cameras, and digital sound recorders in their searches.

A ghost hunter listens for electronic voice phenomena (EVP), evidence of a spirit, in a recording made in a cemetery.

TOSHIBA

XTREME FACT– Ghost hunters often carry GPS units or compasses to help them find their destination and to keep from getting lost.

DANGERS

Ghost hunters sometimes get injured while exploring dangerously neglected buildings and cemeteries. Damaged floors, stairs, and windows often cause falls and cuts. Walking or running on uneven ground can cause sprained ankles and broken bones. Ghost hunters must stay alert to protect themselves from their surroundings.

XTREME FACT– It is possible to be scared to death. When frightened, the human body produces a large amount of adrenaline. This chemical typically helps a person survive a life-threatening situation. However, in a few cases, it may cause the heart to get off rhythm or even stop beating.

HAUNTED HOUSES

Sarah Winchester

G host hunters often seek old, abandoned homes as likely locations for finding spirits. However, well-kept homes may also have ghostly presences. Some call the Winchester Mystery House in San Jose, California, one of the most haunted homes in America.

XTREME FACT– Ghosts of Native Americans, Civil War soldiers, servants, construction workers, and even Sarah Winchester are said to haunt the mansion.

Sarah Winchester was the heir to the Winchester rifle fortune. After her husband and daughter died, a psychic told her that ghosts of people who had been killed by Winchester rifles were seeking revenge for their deaths. The psychic told her to build a house to keep the spirits happy. Sarah's home was under construction from 1884 until her death in 1922. Today, visitors tour the mansion's 160 rooms, secret passages, stairs that go nowhere, and doors that open to walls, all designed by Sarah to keep herself safe from vengeful spirits.

The White House has many stories of hauntings. President Lincoln has reportedly been seen standing at a window, sitting on a bed, and even wandering the hallways. The president's son, Willie, who died in 1862 at the age of 11, is said to still be giggling and running up and down the haunted hallways of the White House.

The attic above the Oval Office has a history of unexplained noises. David Burns, the original owner of the land, is said to haunt the attic. The ghost of William Henry Harrison, the ninth president of the United States, may haunt the attic also. Harrison was the first president to die in office, in 1841, after serving only a month.

XTREME FACT – During the War of 1812, British soldiers set fire to the White House and the U.S. Capitol building. The ghost of a British soldier with a burning torch is said to haunt the White House to this day.

GHOST HOTELS

Hotels are often known for their ghostly guests. The Stanley Hotel in Estes Park, Colorado, is one of the most well-known haunted hotels in North America. Ghost hunters, visitors, and staff members have told of spirited encounters there.

XTREME FACT – Horror novelist Stephen King was inspired to write The Shining *after a stay in the Stanley Hotel. The book was made into a movie in 1980.*

The ghost of **F.O. Stanley**, the hotel's builder and owner, has been spotted in the lobby. His dead wife, Flora, plays the piano in the music room. Elizabeth Wilson, a housekeeper hurt in an accident in Room 217, is said to take special care of guests in that room, unpacking their suitcases and putting items away in drawers.

Bourbon Orleans Hotel is in New Orleans, Louisiana. It features a grand ballroom, a spiral staircase, chandeliers, and ghosts. In the 1800s, the site held a ballroom and theater, as well as a convent, before it became a hotel. Visitors claim to have witnessed the spirits of a little boy and girl, a Confederate soldier, nuns, and a ghost dancer.

XTREME FACT – Haunted hotels often have resident psychics. They try to communicate with the hotel's spirits.

Many people claim to have seen a lone ghost dancer in the Bourbon Orleans Hotel's beautiful ballroom, dancing below the crystal chandeliers.

Haunted Hospitals

Hospitals seem to hold restless spirits. Waverly Hills Sanatorium in Louisville, Kentucky, is an abandoned hospital with stories of paranormal activities. Ghost hunters look for the spirits of nurses and patients, as well as ghosts of a little boy bouncing a ball and a little girl playing hide-and-seek.

Some witnesses hear strange voices, moans, and cries. There are also reports of hot and cold spots, unusual lights, orbs, and shadows. Are they the former residents and staff of the hospital?

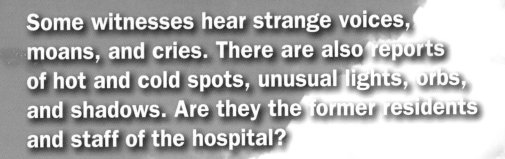

XTREME FACT– Waverly Hills used a tunnel to take away the bodies of dead patients. It was given the nickname "Death Tunnel." People sometimes see a ghostly horse-drawn hearse arriving at the entrance to the tunnel.

West Virginia's Trans-Allegheny Lunatic Asylum was built to care for 250 mentally ill people. However, it often held more than 2,400 patients in its overcrowded halls, resulting in horrible living conditions. Over time, thousands of patients died.

XTREME FACT – *One of the most-reported ghosts in the asylum is a young girl named Lily. She seems to be looking for her mother on the fourth floor.*

The hospital closed in 1994. However, ghostly activities have been reported for decades. Ghost hunters and other visitors have heard screams, whispers, and warnings to leave the hospital. Many experience cold spots and feelings of being touched or pushed.

BATTLEGROUNDS

Gettysburg, Pennsylvania, is often considered the most haunted place in the United States. During the American Civil War, the Battle of Gettysburg was fought on July 1-3, 1863. It was the bloodiest battle ever to take place on American soil.

More than 7,500 Union and Confederate soldiers died at the Battle of Gettysburg in 1863.

Today, the town and battlefield of Gettysburg attract ghost hunters. There are many tales of ghostly Union and Confederate soldiers, some on foot and some on horseback. In addition, the spirits of doctors, nurses, and civilians (adults and children) have been seen or heard by visitors to Gettysburg.

XTREME FACT – During battle, Union soldiers of the 20th Maine Division were led up a hill by a man on a white horse. Most insisted it was the ghost of George Washington.

The Alamo is a fort in today's San Antonio, Texas. In 1836, this fort was the location of a bloody battle between Mexican soldiers and American settlers. After two weeks of fighting, more than 250 Texans were killed, along with nearly 1,500 Mexican soldiers. The Alamo's history of ghostly tales began shortly after the battle.

XTREME FACT – In 1836, right after the battle, Mexican soldiers were ordered to destroy the mission. As they approached the Alamo, they were stopped by a ghostly figure holding a fireball. The soldiers beat a hasty retreat.

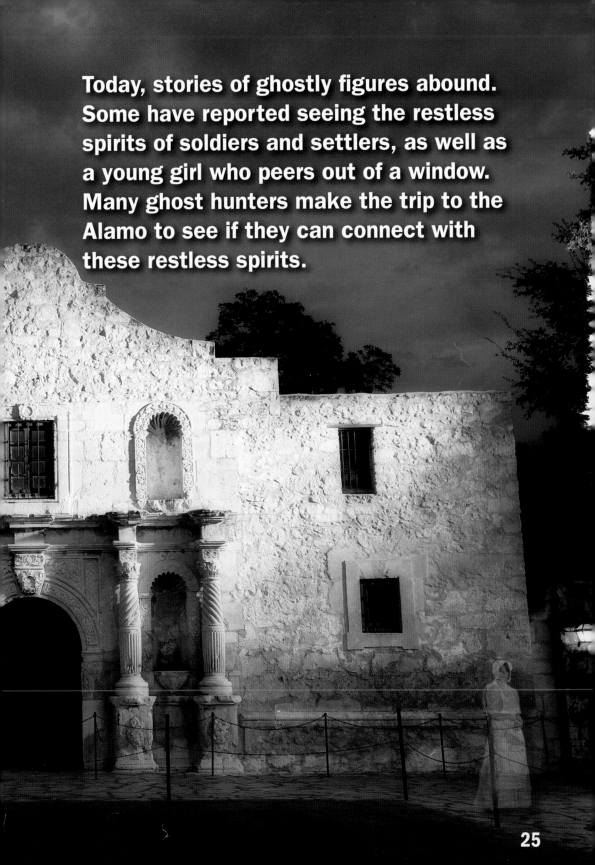

Today, stories of ghostly figures abound. Some have reported seeing the restless spirits of soldiers and settlers, as well as a young girl who peers out of a window. Many ghost hunters make the trip to the Alamo to see if they can connect with these restless spirits.

SHIPS

The *Queen Mary* is a retired British ocean liner first launched in 1934. Today, the ship is a hotel and restaurant moored in Long Beach, California. It is known as "the haunted ship."

The USS *Hornet* is an American aircraft carrier first launched in 1943. The great warship has had many successes, but also several tragedies. More than 300 sailors died on the *Hornet*. Today, the ship is a National Historic Landmark and a museum in Alameda, California. Ghost hunters visit the ship trying to find spectral crewmen.

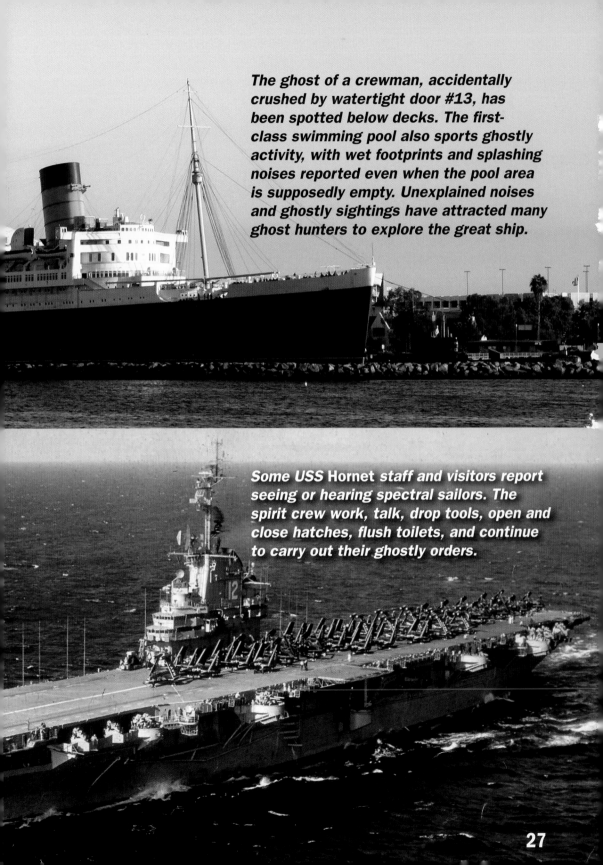

The ghost of a crewman, accidentally crushed by watertight door #13, has been spotted below decks. The first-class swimming pool also sports ghostly activity, with wet footprints and splashing noises reported even when the pool area is supposedly empty. Unexplained noises and ghostly sightings have attracted many ghost hunters to explore the great ship.

Some USS Hornet staff and visitors report seeing or hearing spectral sailors. The spirit crew work, talk, drop tools, open and close hatches, flush toilets, and continue to carry out their ghostly orders.

CEMETERIES

Cemeteries are popular locations for ghost hunting. The St. Louis Cemetery in New Orleans, Louisiana, is well known for its ghostly occupants. The cemetery opened in 1789. Ghosts of past mayors, sailors, Civil War veterans, and even a voodoo priestess are said to appear and disappear before the eyes of the living.

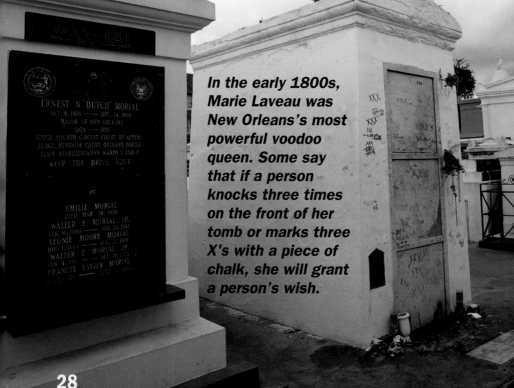

In the early 1800s, Marie Laveau was New Orleans's most powerful voodoo queen. Some say that if a person knocks three times on the front of her tomb or marks three X's with a piece of chalk, she will grant a person's wish.

Hollywood Forever Cemetery is known for its celebrity graves and famous ghosts. Actors Rudolph Valentino, Clifton Webb, Virginia Rappe, as well as the Lady in Black, reportedly haunt the graveyard. For ghost hunters, famous spirits and unknown phantoms create thrilling adventures.

GLOSSARY

ADRENALINE
A chemical created in the human body that is released when a person feels strong emotions such as fear or excitement. Adrenaline causes the heart to beat faster and gives a person quick energy.

CIVIL WAR
The war fought between America's Northern and Southern states from 1861-1865. The Southern states were for slavery. They wanted to start their own country. Northern states fought against slavery and a division of the country.

CONFEDERATE
Someone who fought for the Confederate States of America, which included 11 Southern states that broke away from the United States during the Civil War (1861-1865). The Confederacy ended in 1865 when the war ended and the 11 Confederate states rejoined the United States.

ELECTRONIC VOICE PHENOMENA (EVP)
Sounds found on audio recordings that are believed to be the voices or sounds of ghosts or spirits. EVP may also be caused by static, radio transmissions, and background noise in the area of the recording.

GPS
(GLOBAL POSITIONING SYSTEM)
A system used to pinpoint where a person is located based on satellite tracking.

PARANORMAL
A force or experience that cannot be immediately explained by science.

PSYCHIC
A person who claims to have an extraordinary understanding of, and connection to, supernatural forces and influences, such as ghosts. Also known as a medium or clairvoyant.

SUPERNATURAL
A being, force, or event that defies the laws of nature.

THERMAL SCANNER
A heat-sensitive device that photographically shows the different surface temperatures of whatever it is pointed at. Warmer temperatures are shown in red colors, while cooler temperatures are in blue colors.

INDEX

A

adrenaline 8
Alameda, CA 26
Alamo 24, 25
America (*see also* United States) 10
American settlers 24

B

Bourbon Orleans Hotel 16, 17
Burns, David 13

C

California 10, 26
camera 7
Capitol (building), U.S. 13
Civil War 10, 22, 28
Colorado 14
compass 7
Confederate soldiers 22, 23

D

Death Tunnel 19
digital sound recorder 7

E

electronic voice phenomena (EVP) 7
Estes Park, CO 14

G

Gettysburg (battlefield) 23
Gettysburg, Battle of 22
Gettysburg, PA (town) 22, 23
GPS unit 7

H

Harrison, William Henry 13
Hollywood Forever Cemetery 29
Hornet, USS 26, 27

K

Kentucky 18
King, Stephen 14

L

Lady in Black 29
Laveau, Marie 28
Lily (ghost) 20
Lincoln, Abraham 12
Lincoln, Willie 12
Long Beach, California 26
Louisiana 16, 28
Louisville, KY 18

M

Mexican soldiers 24
motion detector 7

N

National Historic Landmark 26
New Orleans, LA 16, 28
North America 14

O

Oval Office 13

P

Pennsylvania 22
psychic 16

Q

Queen Mary 26

R

Rappe, Virginia 29

S

San Antonio, TX 24
San Jose, CA 10
Shining, The 14
St. Louis Cemetery 28
Stanley, Flora 15
Stanley, F.O. 15
Stanley Hotel 14, 15

T

20th Maine Division 23
Texas 24
thermal scanner 6
thermometer 6
Trans-Allegheny Lunatic Asylum 20, 21

U

Union soldiers 22, 23
United States (*see also* America) 13, 22

V

Valentino, Rudolph 29

W

War of 1812 13
Washington, George 23
Waverly Hills Sanatorium 18, 19
Webb, Clifton 29
West Virginia 20
White House 12, 13
Wilson, Elizabeth 15
Winchester, Sarah 10, 11
Winchester Mystery House 10
Winchester rifle 11